CED 101

A Primer on Identifying and Effectively Addressing Community Needs

Copyright © 2012 New South Consulting, LLC

All rights reserved. Except as permitted under copyright law, no part of this publication may be reproduced, distributed, or transmitted in any form or by any means, or stored in a database or retrieval system, without the prior written permission of the publisher.

New South Consulting, LLC
3911 Inwood Drive
Durham, NC 27705

Visit our website at http://nsconsultingllc.com.

Printed in the United States of America by Lulu Enterprises, Inc. (www.lulu.com)

First Edition: January 2012

ISBN 978-1-105-28109-9

ACKNOWLEDGEMENTS

First and last ... alpha and omega ... beginning and end, I believe any effort I undertake will be in vain if I don't give the ultimate praise to God for allowing me to be a steward of the opportunities and resources I have been blessed to have.

To the one who said "yes" to me more than 15 years ago and has blessed my life ever since – my wife, Kimberly: thank you for encouraging me to keep striving toward my true potential.

To Rachel Angeline and Richard "Allen," my two wonderful children: thank you for keeping me grounded and for your unconditional love.

To Dr. Jim Johnson and Abdul Sm Rasheed, the people who exposed me to the career possibilities of community economic development: thank you for building the platform and for your ongoing guidance.

To Denise Jerrido and Everett Wallace: thank you for offering your expertise and valuable time toward the editing of this text - the breadth of your talents are truly amazing!

To the many CED practitioners I've been blessed to know and work with throughout my career: thank you for your patience with me as I continue to learn the many facets of "God's work."

CONTENTS

Introduction 1

Building on Community Strengths 3
  Anchor Community Institutions (ACIs) 3
    ACI #1: Faith-Based Organizations 4
    ACI #2: Universities 6
    ACI #3: Non-profits 9
    ACI Bonus: "Special" Non-profits 10
  Resources to Explore 11

Getting Started 14
  How Do I Get Started? 14
  The Importance of Being Tax-Exempt 15
  FBO Considerations 17
  Resources to Explore 19

So, What Do You Do? 20
  Assessing Needs – Determining Why 21
  Narrowing Your Focus 23
  Program Development – So THIS is What You Do! 24
  Hitting the Bullseye – Your Target Market 26
  Needs Assessment Revisited 27
  Determining Success – Program Evaluation 29
  Resources to Explore 31

CED and the Law 33
  CED Law Clinics 33

Financial Support 35

Fundraising – Embracing the Challenge *35*
How Much Money Do I Need? *37*
Different Types of Funding *38*
Where Can I Find the Money? *40*
How Do I Get the Money? *41*
Who Can I Call For Help with My Finances? *42*
Resources to Explore *44*

The Importance of Leadership 45
Leadership Styles *46*
Leadership Structures *48*
Resources to Explore *50*

The Personal Side of CED 51

Putting it All Together 53

Bonus Entries 54
A "Kingly" Service (posted on January 17, 2011) *54*
Autism and Economic Development (posted on April 2, 2011) *54*
A "Tragedy" Brewing (posted on March 12, 2011) *55*
Tragedy Averted ... Maybe (posted on April 9, 2011) *57*
What Do Elephants and Poverty Have in Common (posted on April 23, 2011) *57*
Mother's Day Reflections (posted on May 7, 2011) *59*
Labor Day Reflections (posted on September 3, 2011) *60*
Proud Dad (posted on October 8, 2011) *61*

CED 101: A Primer

INTRODUCTION

It appears that in some communities, economic progress occurs "naturally." Nice homes are built, which attract retail shops and schools, which make the community more attractive for businesses to start or to relocate, which bring higher paid employees that purchase the nice homes being built ... and the "circle of economic life" continues.

However, this "natural cycle" has not worked in some communities for many years (even decades)! Whether the cause is urban renewal, segregation/desegregation, income/education gaps, redlining or other economic and social conditions/decisions that were made (and continue to be made), many disadvantaged communities have struggled to grow and prosper economically. In addition, many once prosperous communities have declined in recent years due to urban sprawl as well as the growth of downtown living. Nevertheless, these proud communities have many advantages and assets that can be utilized to jump-start and encourage economic growth and stability.

Efforts to encourage economic growth in disinvested communities have generally been defined as "community economic development." Community economic development (CED) is a term that is understood differently, depending on the person's perspective. Many view CED as affordable housing development ... many say job creation ... or crime prevention ... or better access to health care ... or access to better educational opportunities ... or a higher level of transportation options ... or more access to products and services.

I say CED is all of these and much more! Each community has its own advantages and assets to build upon as well as its own challenges and histories to overcome. There are many success stories of communities that have made positive strides due to the work of many dedicated individuals and organizations.

As in all efforts, the question must be asked "where do I start," which is where this primer can be of assistance. This effort began as a weekly posting on my blog site – New South Blog – covering various topics related to CED. I hope that the information shared in

CED 101: A Primer

this book will help you in determining your community's needs and how to go about addressing them.

I pray that your efforts to revitalize your community are successful. I ask that you pray that this information will be used not just to rebuild communities, but rebuild lives!

Be strong and be blessed!

Richard C. Fuqua

CED 101: A Primer

BUILDING ON COMMUNITY STRENGTHS

Traditionally, economic development has focused on increasing jobs by recruiting companies from City A to City B as well as (to a lesser extent, but with greater emphasis recently) growing jobs from within through entrepreneurship. To support job and population growth, communities have worked to improve all elements of their community, including improving housing stock, improving education, reducing crime, and so on.

However, there are many communities in the U.S., even communities-within-communities, where increasing economic tides don't "raise all boats" equally and when the overall economy "catches a cold," these communities "catch the flu." Many of these communities are disproportionately lower income with higher percentages of people of color. Many suffer with higher unemployment rates, higher rates of crime, lower education levels and other such measures that, when using traditional benchmarks, can make these communities unattractive for future economic investments.

But, as I've seen in many communities I've worked with over the last 15 years, there are many dedicated individuals and organizations working to improve the economic condition of these traditionally disenfranchised communities – and I applaud them! Even with these efforts, I believe there are still "unrealized opportunities" that are hindering these communities from reaching their full potential.

Anchor Community Institutions (ACIs)

Much of these "unrealized opportunities" are due to the existence of what I call "anchor community institutions." Some examples of ACIs include hospitals, existing commercial districts, government centers and others. This primer will highlight three other important ACIs:

- Faith-Based Organizations

- Universities

- Non-profit Organizations

Each word in the phrase provides a wonderful description* of these organizations:

- **"Anchor"** - *something dependable; somebody who or something that provides stability.* These organizations provide stability to communities. In turn, the community looks to them to help affect positive change.

- **"Community"** – *a group of people who live in the same area, or the area in which they live; a group of people with a common background or with shared interests within society.* These organizations are a part of the local community and, in most cases, many individuals in the community are members.

- **"Institution"** – *somebody or something that has been well known and established in a place for a long time.* These organizations provide (or can provide) neighborhood stability because of their longevity as well as their local, regional and/or national organizational infrastructure.

* Definitions courtesy of Encarta® World English Dictionary [North American Edition].

ACI #1: Faith-Based Organizations

Religious institutions of all types have been instrumental in leading positive community economic development (CED) and social change throughout U.S. history (e.g., Quakers in the abolition movement during slavery). In many neighborhoods, the local church serves as a stabilizing force, a place for obtaining assistance, a gathering place, a source for social healing and other worthy roles.

However, many faith-based organizations (FBOs) are facing significant challenges (real or perceived) that threaten their effectiveness, including:

- a greater percentage of the membership that do not live in the local community and, thus, may not have a strong local connection to what happens in the neighborhood after Sunday morning;

- accounts of church leaders being accused of and investigated for misconduct creates mistrust and skepticism for FBOs in general; and

- IRS investigations of numerous FBOs as to whether they "blur the line" between church and other supplementary works, which may threaten the church's tax-exempt status.

Even with these and other challenges, FBOs are looked upon as important partners for CED by local, state and national governments. The White House Office of Faith-Based and Neighborhood Partnerships is an example of the importance of these organizations.

With the needs so great and resources becoming more and more scarce, here are a few recommendations for FBOs to be more effective in their CED efforts:

1. **Get organized.** If you are doing (or plan to do) works such as building affordable housing, job creation efforts, commercial development and other CED, establish an independent, non-profit organization that can carry out these works and is, also, tax-exempt (if applicable). You will better protect the church's tax-exempt status as well as be in a better position to raise money through foundations and other grant making bodies.

2. **Get together.** Whether your FBO is large or small, find other organizations with similar missions and partner with them to increase access to resources as well as to "share the burden" (Galatians 6:2). There's strength in numbers (e.g., building of the Tower of Babel)!

3. **Get busy.** The first step in this process is having and expressing the vision (Proverbs 29:18). The next steps can be much more difficult – trusting God and putting a strategy in

place to realize the vision. It is in this stage that partnerships are formed, organizations are strengthened, and processes are implemented.

A book I would recommend that goes into more depth about the challenges and opportunities of FBOs is entitled *Crisis in the Village: Restoring Hope in African-American Communities* by Robert M. Franklin.

ACI #2: Universities

In the previous section I discussed the opportunities that faith-based organizations have to positively affect community economic development (CED). This section will highlight another "anchor institution" – universities.

The original Latin word *"universitas"* was used to describe specialized "associations of students and teachers with collective legal rights usually guaranteed by charters issued by princes, prelates, or the towns in which they were located."[i] Some of the first universities were established as early as 425 AD.

Fast forward to today and we see that universities are at the forefront of teaching not only specialized skills, but how to think critically. Each day, thousands of students and faculty create "mini-cities" where learning happens and, more relevantly, commerce happens. The surrounding community is affected – positively and negatively – by these institutions, intentionally or not. For some, positive contributions have been accomplished in partnership with the local community (e.g., business creation, housing, etc.).

However, in many instances, the university and the local community are at odds with each other, creating an adversarial "town vs. gown" relationship rather than a partnership. When a university does not see the importance of working with the local community for mutually beneficial ends, it creates isolation and ill-feelings on both sides.

There are numerous examples of universities that have worked with local government and community leaders to create jobs, build affordable housing, and perform other successful CED activities. One such example is given below:

- Marquette University/New West Side Comprehensive Plan (Milwaukee, WI)[ii]:

    Revitalizing Marquette University's immediate neighborhood and beyond is the long-term goal of a diverse community group, including the university, neighborhood associations and other key stakeholders. That revitalization goal is clearly outlined in the Near West Side Comprehensive Plan. In the 1990's, Marquette initiated the Campus Circle Project that invested more than $50 million in the area. More recently, Marquette has partnered with community leaders, government entities and other stakeholders to transform an underutilized square city block of asphalt into a desirable, green, usable community park; focusing economic development resources through the Main Street Milwaukee Program on 27th Street, arguably the most depressed retail corridor in the city; and transforming 180,000+ square feet of a former, unused hospital into 99 trendy, loft-style apartments.

    "Marquette recognizes that our job in the neighborhood isn't over yet. This time around, it's not a solo act for Marquette. We're in a model partnership with neighborhood groups, the city of Milwaukee and other key stakeholders to bring about positive change," according to Carol Winkel, Marquette's director of governmental and community relations.

Universities that are located in low-wealth and/or disinvested communities are in a unique position to leverage their "anchor" position to affect positive change. For example, academic institutions such as Historically Black Colleges and Universities (HBCUs) are, for the most part, strategically positioned due to their historical significance (HBCUs date back to the 1830's, with most being established before 1964) and the location of the majority of their campuses in low-wealth communities.

There are many resources that HBCUs and similar institutions can draw upon, including funding/technical assistance (HUD's Office of University Partnerships) as well as many other individuals/ organizations who desire to assist HBCUs and similar institutions to build their communities while strengthening their respective campuses.

One of the many examples of successful HBCU/community partnerships involves Howard University and the surrounding Washington DC area. Howard received a three-year Historically Black Colleges and Universities Grant in 2006 from the U.S. Department of Housing and Urban Development to support Manna, Inc. rehabilitation of a 12-unit affordable condominium project in Northwest Washington, D.C.; support a residential façade rehabilitation program in the Deanwood/Burrville neighborhoods in Ward 7 in Northeast Washington, DC.; establish a microloan program to businesses in the Shaw neighborhood; extend a pilot training program currently implemented under the HUD Universities Rebuilding America Program in New Orleans to the Lower Ninth Ward, training homeowners and contractors in environmentally-safe renovation and repair work practices; remodel the Community Learning Center to create a single large classroom suitable for enlarged community classes; and remodel the interior of the Mary Church Terrell home and strengthen associated structures for public use, making the historic structure conform more precisely to its historic vernacular.[iii]

Some key elements of a successful university/community partnership include the following:

- Engaged leadership at the top of and throughout each stakeholder organization (e.g., community leaders, president/chancellor, etc.);

- A broad base of involvement within the local community;

- A thorough knowledge-base of resources, both local, state and federal; and

- A desire to build something positive (MOST IMPORTANT).

My desire is that more HBCUs and similar organizations embrace their community importance and that they take a more aggressive stance in driving positive change instead of being reactive or, even worse, disengaged.

ACI #3: Non-profits

The third type of "anchor institution" I would like to highlight is the "non-profit organization." As with faith-based institutions and universities written about previously, non-profits are important components in community economic development. True to their name, non-profits are organizations whose primary mission is other than making a profit. Some mission examples include providing affordable housing, job creation, education our youth, feeding the homeless, and others. Some are large and very established (e.g., American Heart Association) and some are very small (which is the case for most non-profits).

As with the other two "anchor institutions," the local community and the government look to non-profits to lead efforts in providing much-needed services to the disenfranchised. However, many non-profits struggle to survive day-to-day due to a number of factors, including the lack of financial resources, "mission creep," the overall economy, leadership capacity, and others.

According to GuideStar, a national organization that gathers and publicizes information about non-profit organizations, the four main areas to measure a non-profit organization's effectiveness are as follows:

- Mission

- Impact and Customer/Public Satisfaction

- Planning and Self-Assessment

- Business Measures (e.g., how many people are actually served, cost to deliver per service unit, etc.)

It is interesting that the GuideStar list did NOT include an organization's financials as a top measure of effectiveness. Other ways that non-profits can become more effective include the following:

- Development of Board Leadership – The board of directors is the heart and soul of the organization and can "make or break" it. If the board is not strong in its belief of the organization, diverse in its experience, and dedicated to the overall health of the organization, the non-profit will become ineffective and irrelevant.

- Partnership Development – With scarce resources, it is vital that non-profits find ways to partner with organizations with complementary missions to reach their goals. In fact, foundations and other grant makers require this from organizations seeking funding.

I believe that if a non-profit focuses on the items listed above, the money will follow.

Much of my career has centered on working with and/or providing services to non-profit organizations. I believe in their importance as well as their impact on communities.

It is my hope that the three "anchor institutions" I've highlighted will seek to do more to lead community economic development efforts locally, regionally, and nationally.

ACI Bonus: "Special" Non-profits

I have spoken about the non-profit organization as an "anchor institution" referring to its importance in leading community economic development efforts. I will highlight some types of non-profits whose primary focus is promoting and enhancing CED.

Community Development Corporations (CDCs) – CDCs are non-profit, community-based organizations that anchor capital locally through the development of both residential and commercial property, ranging from affordable housing to developing shopping centers and even owning businesses. First formed in the 1960s, they have expanded rapidly in size and numbers since. An industry survey published in 2006 found that 4,600 CDCs promote community economic stability by developing over 86,000 units of affordable housing and 8.75 million square feet of commercial and industrial space a year.[iv] There are successful CDCs associated with faith-based institutions (e.g., Abyssinian Development Corporation in Harlem), universities (e.g., Benedict-Allen CDC in Columbia, SC) as well as community-based (e.g., Mountain Housing Opportunities in Asheville, NC; Accion USA in New York, NY; Chicanos Por La Causa in Arizona).

Community Development Financial Institutions (CDFIs) – CDFIs are financial institutions which provide credit and financial services to underserved markets and populations, primarily in the USA but also in the UK. A CDFI may be a community development bank, a community development credit union (CDCU), a community development loan fund (CDLF), a community development venture capital fund (CDVC), a microenterprise development loan fund, or a community development corporation (how about that!).[v] Nationwide, over 1,000 CDFIs serve economically distressed communities by providing credit, capital and financial services that are often unavailable from mainstream financial institutions. Some examples of successful CDFIs include the Center for Community Self-Help (based in Durham, NC), NCCDI Capital (based in Raleigh, NC), and ShoreBank (based in Chicago, IL).

So many success stories have been, and are being, written daily by these and other institutions that it would take many books to record them and I could not adequately give them their just due. However, I will attempt to provide brief glimpses into their work to encourage you to seek them out OR to start your own local efforts.

Resources to Explore

Faith-Based Organizations

- White House Office of Faith-Based and Neighborhood Partnerships - (http://www.whitehouse.gov/administration/eop/ofbnp)

- *Crisis in the Village* by Robert M. Franklin - (http://search.barnesandnoble.com/Crisis-in-the-Village/Robert-M-Franklin/e/9780800638870/)

University/Community Partnerships

- Office of University Partnership (HUD) - (http://www.oup.org/)
- Duke University Community Engagement - (https://community.duke.edu/)
- UNC Community-Campus Partnership - (http://www.sog.unc.edu/programs/ccp/)

Non-Profits

- BoardSource (assistance with non-profit boards) - (http://www.boardsource.org/)
- GuideStar - (http://www2.guidestar.org/)
- National Council of Nonprofits - (http://www.councilofnonprofits.org/)

Community Development Corporations

- Local Initiatives Support Corporation (LISC) - (http://www.lisc.org/)
- National Alliance of Community Economic Development Associations - (http://www.naceda.org/)
- North Carolina Association of CDCs - (http://www.ncacdc.org/)

   NOTE: *Many other states have their own statewide association.*

Community Development Financial Institutions (CDFIs)

- CDFI Fund (United States Department of the Treasury) - (http://www.cdfifund.gov/)
- Coalition of Community Development Financial Institutions - (http://www.cdfi.org/)

- Center for Community Self-Help - (http://www.self-help.org/)
- North Carolina Community Development Initiative Capital - (http://ncinitiative.org/)
- Opportunity Finance Network - (http://www.opportunityfinance.net/)

GETTING STARTED

Building a firm foundation for your organization is just as important as blocking and tackling is to football. It will allow you to proceed more confidently in meeting the needs of your community.

In this section, we'll discuss various topics pertaining to your organization's start-up activities, including:

- Obtaining a tax-exempt designation
- Becoming an "official" organization
- Resources that can assist you
- Considerations of faith-based organizations

How Do I Get Started?

"An idea that is developed and put into action is more important than an idea that exists only as an idea." – Gautama Buddha

You've noticed a great need in your community (e.g., teen unemployment, crime, obesity, etc.) and have come up with a great idea to address that need or would like to implement an existing program in your neighborhood. As mentioned previously, a firm foundation for your organization, through which your idea will be implemented, is of highest importance. If you plan to raise funds from outside sources, for example, the decisions made at this stage will determine where you can go to raise needed funds.

Organization Type – There are two primary choices for organization type: for-profit and non-profit. As the names suggest, each type is driven by its primary objective. For-profit organizations exist to maximize profits (revenues minus expenses) for its owners and/or shareholders. In contrast, non-profits are not PRIMARILY motivated by profits, but rather by fulfilling its charitable mission. However, there are instances where you can find both types of organizations mutually benefitting each other (e.g., a for-profit organization creating a related non-profit organization to perform charitable work such as the Ford Foundation). Keep in mind that foundations and some government programs can only award grants to tax-exempt non-profit organizations (we'll talk about becoming tax-exempt soon).

Organization Name – It has been said that "words have meaning and names have power."[vi] Don't underestimate the importance of choosing a name for your organization that communicates who you are, what you do, and/or who you serve (e.g., American Cancer Society). In choosing a name, you need to make sure that the proposed name is not being used by another organization. You can contact your secretary of state and local registrar to check the availability of a name.

In order to become an official organization, you would submit an application or articles of incorporation to your secretary of state or similar entity. In addition, you may be required to apply for a business license in your local jurisdiction. Check with your state and local governments for their specific requirements for creating your organization.

The Importance of Being Tax-Exempt

There's a lot of discussion going on these days about taxes – whether to increase them or reduce them, how to spend them, and so forth. However, there is one item in the tax laws that I hope NEVER goes away – Section 501 of the Internal Revenue Code. What is this you might ask? Well, I'm glad you asked! Section 501 describes organizations that are exempt from taxation. You may have heard of the term "501(c)(3) organizations," which describes many of the non-profit organizations we're most familiar with. The following briefly describes the process of becoming tax-exempt.

Before I go on, let's make sure there's an understanding of the difference between being a non-profit organization and being tax-exempt. According to the Internal Revenue Service (IRS), non-profit status is a state law concept. Non-profit status may make an organization eligible for certain benefits, such as **state** sales, property and income tax exemptions. Although most federal tax-exempt organizations are non-profit organizations, organizing as a non-profit organization at the state level does not <u>automatically</u> grant the organization exemption from **federal** income tax. Therefore, you must not only become certified as a non-profit organization in your state, but you must apply to the IRS to become federally tax-exempt.

<u>What are the benefits of becoming tax-exempt?</u> The two primary benefits of becoming tax-exempt are as follows [1]:

- **Donations to the non-profit are tax-deductible.** With 501(c)(3) non-profits, donations are tax-deductible to the donor.

- **Access to grants earmarked for 501(c)(3)s.** Certain grants and other public allocations are only available to 501(c)(3) organizations.

<u>Is there a fee associated with the application?</u> The application fee will depend on your anticipated "annual gross receipts" (AGR) – either a fee of $400 for AGR of less than $10,000 during the preceding 4 years OR $850 for AGR of greater than or equal to $10,000 during the preceding 4 years (as of September 2011).

<u>What is the application process?</u>

- Obtain non-profit status from your state;

- Obtain an Employee Identification Number; and

- Complete and submit Form 1023 (for most organizations) along with supplemental documentation and appropriate fee to the IRS. **NOTE:** This process can be a significant investment of time, depending on the amount of work that has already been done (e.g., budget, detailed description of organization and programming, etc.).

There are many organizations that assist groups with completing this application for free or for a nominal fee; however, it is not necessary.

FBO Considerations

When it comes to non-profits and their tax-exempt status, faith-based organizations (FBOs) must be especially careful when they decide to go beyond "having church" to providing services that benefit the community overall. For example, care must be taken when a FBO goes from developing Sunday School curriculum for its own use to developing and selling biblical children's stories to be used by the general public ... or when a FBO expands its transitional housing efforts from housing the homeless in their multi-purpose building to providing shelter in homes the FBO has purchased ... or when a FBO intends to purchase land not just for a new church building but for other uses such as senior housing and small-shop retail...and the list can go on.

Even though the examples given above can be deemed as extensions of the FBO's overall mission, these "extensions" may be viewed by the Internal Revenue Service differently. In fact, there are many recent examples of FBOs and their leaders being investigated by the federal government questioning their tax-exempt status. Ultimately, these investigations were dropped, but the fact remains that as budgets tighten at the federal and state levels, government bodies will continue to aggressively seek additional sources of revenue and FBOs will continue to be potential targets as the line blurs between their charitable and auxiliary activities.

One way to address this possibility is for FBOs to establish independent organizations that can facilitate these activities without jeopardizing the FBOs tax-exempt status. For example, using the "bible children's stories" example from above, I recommend that the FBO create a separate entity (e.g., a publishing company) that would develop, market and sell the products so that the tax-exempt status of the FBO would not be put into question – especially when the income of the publishing company begins to increase substantially. In addition, if the FBO intends to secure grants for various charitable activities that will benefit the community as a whole, many philanthropic organizations cannot award grants directly to FBOs, but can make awards to non-profit organizations that facilitate these charitable activities.

The examples given above are merely for illustration and not intended to be definitive. Case law is constantly evolving in this area, so please consult with a local attorney or CPA who can help you wade through these waters. If you have questions or comments that would help broaden this discussion, please respond.

FBO Highlight – Community Anchors Limited
During the Civil Rights Movement, religious institutions played a key role in shaping social change and pricking social consciousness. The history of what lead to the Movement as well as the "struggle" in its aftermath continues even today in many communities. One example of this phenomenon is the issue of "diversity-based school assignment" versus "neighborhood schools" being played out in Wake County (NC) schools (as of the fall 2011). An example of where a church is working with the local community to overcome a history of racial hatred and bias involves the Town of Clayton and Mount Vernon Christian Church (MVCC).

Located southeast of Raleigh, NC, Clayton has had a long history with and became known as one of the centers of Ku Klux Klan activity. MVCC, established in 1898, has a long and storied history in the local community and continues that tradition under the leadership of Dr. Terence Leathers.

When ConAgra's Slim Jim plant located in Garner exploded in 2009, many MVCC members were affected. It also exposed the lack of preparedness in the community, especially the black community, for dealing with disaster.

In response, Dr. Leathers created Community Anchors Limited (CAL), an organization that provides emergency management training, in partnership with local fire/EMS departments, for communities that have historically been overlooked (e.g., minority communities). As a result of CAL's work, Dr. Leathers has established formal partnerships with the Town of Clayton and its Fire and Police Departments and has sought grants for CAL and MVCC in partnership with these entities. With the Town's history as mentioned above, these are historic events!

For more information on CAL and their work, their website is http://communityanchorsltd.org/.

This is just one example of how faith-based organizations (FBOs) continue to provide leadership for social change and community economic development.

Resources to Explore

- Internal Revenue Service (becoming tax exempt) - (http://www.irs.gov/charities/charitable/article/0,,id=96099,00.html)
- Society of Nonprofit Organizations (starting a non-profit) - (http://www.snpo.org/resources/startup.php)

So, What Do You Do?

Even though this question is asked of you often, it will also be asked about the work of your organization. As a community economic development (CED) organization, the answer to this question could be broad or narrowly focused, specific or general...and can mean the difference between receiving a response of "Oh, ok" or "Tell me more." From potential volunteers to prospective donors to possible board members, each want to know if what you do is in line with their interests and priorities.

In the non-profit arena, the more formal term used to define "what you do" is call "programming." Your organization was created to fulfill some need, advocate for positive change, and/or improve the overall community. The specific ways you accomplish this is through the creation and implementation of programs. If you look at organizations as diverse as the Autism Speaks, NAACP or Trickle Up, each has created programs and activities that support the organization's mission and vision. For your organization to be success, you will need to spend time developing the ability to clearly articulate what you do and why you do it.

Before addressing how to more clearly define your organization's programming, there is one important "DO NOT" to consider – DO NOT create programming just to apply for a particular grant. There are many, many funding options with a diverse array of funding priorities and it is highly likely that "one is right for you." So, be true to your organization's mission and vision!

In order to confidently articulate what you do and why, the following questions should be answered (not an exhaustive list):

1. How do you know there is a need (or demand) for the program you want to do?

2. How will your program address these needs?

3. Are there other organizations in the community addressing these needs and how?

4. Who are you reaching with your program? What is your target market?

5. What resources do you need to implement the program?

6. How will you know whether the program is successful?

The ultimate measure of your organization's worth is its ability to successfully address the needs that have been identified.

Assessing Needs – Determining Why

One of the first steps in answering the question "So, what do you do?" is determining what needs your programming addresses. We can provide anecdotal evidence for a number of worthy efforts, whether it's alleviating poverty, increasing school graduation rates, reducing obesity in children, or a host of others. However, when it comes to securing financial and human resources, expressing anecdotal evidence may not be enough to be successful. Performing a formal "needs assessment" is a key element in determining community needs.

A needs assessment is "a process for determining and addressing needs, or 'gaps' between current conditions and desired conditions, often used for improvement in individuals, education/training, organizations, or communities. The need can be a desire to improve current performance or to correct a deficiency."[vii] Many organizations perform these assessments on an ongoing basis in a variety of areas, including universities (e.g., student population growth), chambers of commerce (e.g., business needs), and municipalities (e.g., population growth patterns), with the goal of determining how to best allocate scarce resources for desired outcomes. In community economic development, the goals (and methods used for determining need) are similar.

Important Tip:

Narrow your focus (you can't be all things to all people)!

For example, you have an interest in addressing childhood obesity in the African-American community. You've witnessed an increase in the number of children who are overweight and want to do something about it. So, you create a non-profit organization and begin to speak with companies and foundations about the possibility of funding your efforts. You quickly learn that some have experience in funding efforts like this and ask you specific questions, such as:

- How many children in your target area are obese?

- What are the demographics of those who are most at risk?

- Are there other organizations in your community addressing the same need?

- What are the long-term effects of not addressing obesity in African-American children?

As you ponder these and other questions, you may ask "How can I get answers to these questions?" For this subject, there is a wealth of information and statistics that can be used, including information from the Centers for Disease Control, the U. S. Department of Health and Human Services (Office of Minority Health), as well as your local county health department. However, depending on the subject, you may have to develop your own statistical data using other means, such as surveys and focus groups.

Whatever data sources you use, make sure that the data is up-to-date and relevant for your assessment and that your sources are credible (e.g., government data). The more up-to-date and relevant your data sources are, the more confident you will be in determining and explaining "why."

Narrowing Your Focus

Continuing the theme of answering the question "So, what do you do?," after you've researched the needs in your community and narrowed the needs you plan to address based on the goals and objectives of the organization, the process of developing a strategy to address those needs can begin. Note that before you begin addressing the needs, you must FOCUS your energies on the SPECIFIC needs you plan to address. No organization can be ALL things to ALL people and address ALL the needs in a particular community. For example, the causes and effects of homelessness are diverse and far-reaching. Nevertheless, there are many organizations that have been created to address different "layers" of homelessness, including affected populations (e.g., veterans and children), addictions, and so on.

You might ask the question of how one can narrow the scope of one's work to address community needs. There are a number of ways this can be accomplished, including:

- Your personal interests – Your passion to do the work will go a long way towards its success. Let's say you have a passion for music and want to help at-risk youth become better students, you could create an organization that exposes young people to classical music and, even, create a youth orchestra. Your case would be strengthened if you found in your research that exposure to the arts leads to better grades and that educational funding for these activities is being reduced.

- The skills/interest of your board – An extension of the previous point, narrowing your scope will be much easier if your board members are passionate about how to address a specific community need and have the skills, contacts, etc. to add value to the effort.

- Unique opportunities – Even though I've mentioned previously that an organization should not create programming just to "chase the money," there are times when the "stars are aligned" and that funding opportunities help to "open the mind to other possibilities." For example, the North Carolina Fund was created in the early 1960's as a "laboratory" to address poverty and became as a precursor to the nation's War on Poverty. The Fund requested proposals from communities throughout North Carolina as to how they would address poverty in their locales. For many, this was a once-in-a-lifetime opportunity that provided a catalyst for creating unique programming to address an issue that had plagued their communities for decades. As a result, the evolution of many of these organizations and their efforts are still in effect today.

Narrowing your focus cannot be overstated. There are many organizations that have found themselves unable to attract funding or other needed resources because they were (or at least perceived to be) too broad in scope. Find your niche!

Program Development – So THIS is What You Do!

What you offer for the betterment of the community, specifically your programming, is the "heart and soul" of any non-profit organization. After you've assessed the needs of the community and matched them with your and/or your board's "work passion," you are in a position to develop your organization's programming.

There are numerous decisions that need to be made, including:

- Specific services you will offer (e.g., tutoring, financial education, advocacy, technical assistance, etc.);

- Who will offer these services (e.g., volunteers, staff, in partnership with other organizations, etc.);

- Method(s) of offering services (e.g., web-based, one-on-one, in group settings, audio/video, etc.);

- To whom will the services be offered (your target market(s);

- Location(s) for providing services (e.g., in the client's home, in a church fellowship hall, at the library, in a public park, etc.);

- Marketing methods (e.g., public service announcements, paid advertising, posting flyers at the local community center, word-of-mouth, etc.);

- How to measure success; and

- Service fees or other charges.

As an example, to address the lack of exposure to the arts that has been determined to contribute to the achievement gap found in at-risk youth, you have decided to create an "arts academy." This academy will provide exposure to a variety of arts (e.g., music, visual, dance, etc.) for young people free of charge in partnership with the local parks and recreation department, students at the local college, and industry artists who have "made it big." Sessions will be held on Saturdays at local churches and community centers. Advertising will be done through the local public access channel; flyers posted at barber shops, beauty salons and grocery stores; and announcements at churches in the area.

For those with a business background, these items sound eerily familiar to elements of a traditional business plan. And you would be right! In essence, most of our discussions have focused on the development of your non-profit BUSINESS! Even though you are, or will be, providing products and services that in many circles would be considered "charitable," the foundation undergirding your efforts is a BUSINESS and should be viewed and managed like one, including asking questions like (1) How do I generate revenues to sustain my efforts? (2) How can I most efficiently offer my products/services? (3) Who will perform the accounting function of the organization's finances? ...and so on.

Back to program development... The answers to the questions posed earlier will drive many other decisions, including the amount of money you will need at each stage of program execution, the human capacity you will need, what other partner organizations you will need to establish relationships with, and others.

Speaking of "partner organizations," we will focus on this important element in the development of your programming.

Hitting the Bullseye – Your Target Market

As you develop your organization's programming, who you are attempting to reach is just as important as what you will do when you reach them. One would think that the "what" (your programming) is meant for a particular "who" (your target market). However, this can be one of the hardest decisions to make because, invariably, when you target your efforts to a specific population or demographic, you are excluding other populations or demographics (and you don't like leaving anyone out!). However, this decision will help to narrow your focus and help to identify potential partners in delivering your programming.

The term "target market" has traditionally been used in business circles, but its use has become more and more commonplace in the non-profit world. According to Encarta® World English Dictionary, a *target market* is "a group of customers of a type considered likely to buy a particular product." Let's break this down within our context:

- "a group of customers…" – The number of persons you're trying to reach is as important in "non-profit world" as it is in the for-profit arena. In business, investors want to maximize their return on investment. In philanthropy, contributors want to know that their donation has as broad a reach as possible. In addition, just like for-profits who want to reduce cost and increase efficiency in the delivery of products or services, the more people your services can reach SHOULD reduce your cost-per-person served, depending on how your services are delivered (e.g., one-on-one versus group settings).

- "…of a type considered likely to buy…" – Will a person living in a desert region want to purchase a fur coat? Not likely. Would a 15-year old desire to have a cell phone? Highly likely. These two examples highlight the fact that the product or service you offer should meet the needs and wants of a particular group of people. For example, if it has been determined that a community is in need of more affordable housing, consideration should be given to the quality of housing, not just the bottom-line cost of development. Individuals want to live in housing that safe, decent, and sanitary AND that they can be proud of. "Affordable" does (and should) not mean "cheap."

- "...a particular product." – As we've mentioned before, it is impossible to be all things to all people. Your "product" may be tutoring...or housing development...or health care...or providing volunteers – whatever your "product" is, strive to be the BEST!

As you decide who you're trying to reach, this will help you to make other decisions such as how to reach them (marketing), who can help (partners), and so on.

Needs Assessment Revisited

Let's see...we've talked about assessing the needs of your community and matching these needs with your organization's interests. After assessing community needs, you would develop programming to address these needs. We've talked about the importance of focusing your efforts to avoid trying to be all things to all people. We've discussed the reasoning behind and necessity of knowing your target market (in other words, who you're trying to reach to positively affect their lives in some way). Now, let's look at "needs assessment" from a different vantage point - what are the needs of YOUR ORGANIZATION to most effectively serve your target market with your programming.

When one begins to look at the needs of an organization, the focus usually sharpens very quickly on MONEY. Now don't get me wrong, having sufficient financial resources are vital for short- and long-term success, but it is not the first thing you need and it may not even be the most important! As has been mentioned before, having the right PEOPLE on the team, I submit, is more important than money. People help create the organization in its infancy…people can perform a preliminary community needs assessment…people develop the organization's programming concepts…people help identify the MONEY!

To expand this idea further, an organizational needs assessment should include answering the following questions:

- Do we have the "right" board members? Even though your board is enthusiastic and supportive, the experience and skill sets of the members may be very similar (e.g., members of the same church, neighbors, etc.) – on the surface, of course. However, as you look at the make-up of your board, seek to identify members with experience in areas such as finance/accounting, management, legal, working with your target market(s), public relations, fundraising, city/county government, advocacy, and others. Resources that can help include organizations such as Triangle BoardConnect (to identify potential board members) and BoardSource (to build the board's capacity).

- How many volunteers do we need? As you implement your programming, you cannot solely rely on board members to do the work. You will need dedicated volunteers for program implementation and, ultimately, to become advocates and ambassadors on behalf of the organization. (Possible resources: United Way, Volunteer Match, and Senior Corps).

- Are there other organizations in the community I can work with and how can I work with them? You will learn about other organizations that do similar work and/or target similar markets as you perform your community needs assessment. You will, also, get vital information from your board members because, in many cases, they are very familiar with these organizations and may even serve on their boards as well. Feel free to reach out to these organizations to let them know what you plan to do, seek their advice and explore possible partnership opportunities.

- How much money do I need and where can I find it? You will need to determine your organizational and programming budget(s) as well as develop a strategy for securing these financial resources. We'll discuss this important topic in the near future.

You will find that by doing a thorough organizational needs assessment, you will identify YOUR needs to effective implement your programming that will address COMMUNITY needs.

Determining Success – Program Evaluation

You have spent countless hours creating your organization's programming to meet a need in your community. You've developed key partnerships and your board is top-shelf. Now you're ready to approach funders for support – but wait, there's more! How will you know if what you've spent time developing will be successful? In order to determine whether investments of time, money and energy were worth it, an evaluation of the program should be planned and performed.

Important Tip:

Think about you will evaluate your program BEFORE starting your program!

It has been said that "(a) true measure of your worth includes all the benefits others have gained from your success."[viii] Taking this thought a step further, there should be an objective way to account for these "benefits" so that the value (or "worth") can be better determined.

Program evaluation is an important step in a program's life cycle and it must be deliberately planned **on the front end** of the planning process. Most, if not all, funders want to know how you propose to measure success. Key questions that should be asked when determining how to evaluate your program include the following:

- What are the *desired outcomes* of this program? What are the goals? What are we trying to accomplish within the next month/quarter/year(s)?

- How will we get there? What *activities* will enable us to reach our outcomes?

- What will *indicate* to us that we are making progress toward the desired outcomes?

Nevertheless, even if you are already implementing your program, for evaluation purposes it is essential to identify and document the program *outcomes*, *activities*, and *indicators* that will be evaluated. Think of the desired **outcomes** as *what you ultimately want the program to accomplish*, the **activities** as *what you will do to get there*, and the **indicators** as *the gauge of whether, and to what degree, you are making progress*.[ix]

Outcomes should be consistent with what could reasonably be accomplished and not "pie in the sky." This doesn't mean you won't strive for more, but in terms of carrying out an evaluation the more clearly defined and measurable the outcome, the better. For example, your outcome may be to reduce the high school drop-out rate among Hispanic students or to increase the number of African-American girls majoring in engineering.

The *activities* are the interventions that your program will provide in order to bring about the intended outcomes. In general, program activities can be defined as any type of direct service or information that is provided to participants. Continuing with the above example targeting African-American girls, you may provide direct tutoring services and mentoring opportunities to encourage more interest in the engineering fields.

Indicators act as the gauge of whether, and to what degree, your program is making progress. Your program's progress needs to be examined in two distinct ways:

1. the quantity and quality of the **program activities you are delivering**, and

2. the quantity and quality of the **outcomes that your program is achieving**.

For example, one indicator may be to "increase the number of African-American girls successfully passing advanced math classes in high school by 50% over the next three years."

Equally important in this discussion are what information is being captured and how you capture information for evaluation. If you are measuring progress for a particular indicator, you would want to determine the "base line" by obtaining data at the beginning of the program (e.g., how many African-American girls are successfully passing advanced math classes now). In addition, consider using methods such as focus groups, surveys, and pre-/post-tests to capture relevant data.

As mentioned before, the more detailed you are in planning and executing program evaluation, the more confident you will be in communicating your program's success (which could lead to increase support of your efforts).

Resources to Explore

Needs Assessment Tools/Information

- Writing a Needs Assessment - (http://teacher.scholastic.com/products/fundingconnection/grant_resources/guidance_samples/pdfs/Writing_Grant_Needs.pdf)
- Community Needs Assessment Guide - (http://www.luc.edu/curl/pdfs/A_Community_Needs_Assessment_Guide_.pdf)

Statistics

- American FactFinder - (http://factfinder2.census.gov/faces/nav/jsf/pages/index.xhtml)
- Community development research and statistics (HUD) - (http://www.huduser.org/portal/)
- Crime Statistics - (https://www.crimereports.com/)

Program Evaluation

- Article on program evaluation - (http://ezinearticles.com/?Five-Simple-Steps-to-Evaluate-Your-Program&id=6814141)
- Tools - (http://www.programevaluation.org/tools.htm)

CED AND THE LAW

Even before programs such as the Community Development Block Grant (CDBG) program was enacted by Congress in 1974, the federal government had been intricately involved in creating policy and funding programs that benefitted low-, medium- and moderate-income individuals and families. These programs sought to address many of the social and economic challenges of these populations such as blight, poverty, unemployment, lack of affordable housing, etc.

However, another vital piece of the puzzle that is often overlooked is the important role the legal system plays in shaping and implementing CED. From the NAACP and other civil rights organizations to public and private practices to university-based law clinics (talked about more below), these organizations work to address a wide variety of issues that affect CED, including family law, poverty law, government benefits, homelessness, housing and legal assistance to the poor.

CED Law Clinics

There is a wide array of law clinics throughout the U.S. that focus on community economic development. Even though each may have a different focus (e.g., affordable housing, entrepreneurship, etc.), they are all dedicated to improving the economic conditions of low wealth populations through the law by providing direct services as well as specialized training for future lawyers. Some examples of CED law clinics include the following:

- Duke University
  (http://www.law.duke.edu/ced/)

- Florida A&M University
  (http://law.famu.edu/go.cfm/do/Page.View/pid/83)

- George Washington University
  (http://www.law.gwu.edu/Academics/EL/clinics/SBCED/Pages/Overview.aspx)

- North Carolina Central University
  (http://law.nccu.edu/clinics/small-business/)

- Syracuse University
  (http://www.law.syr.edu/academics/clinical-legal-education/community-development-law-clinic/)

- University of Alabama
  (http://www.law.ua.edu/academics/law-clinics/community-development-clinic/)

- UCLA
  (http://www.law.ucla.edu/centers-programs/clinical-program/in-house-clinics/Pages/community-economic-development-clinic.aspx)

- UNC – Chapel Hill
  (http://www.law.unc.edu/academics/clinic/cdl/default.aspx)

- Vanderbilt University
  (http://law.vanderbilt.edu/academics/clinical-legal-education/index.aspx)

- Yale University
  (http://www.law.yale.edu/academics/NonprofitOrganizationsClinic.htm)

If you have legal questions regarding your small business, if your landlord has treated you unfairly or have other issues affecting your economic wellbeing, contact your local CED law clinic for assistance.

As you can see, CED and the legal profession are "joined at the hip." The community must ensure that the legal profession continues this service without bias that benefits ALL people.

For a more exhaustive list of university law clinics, visit the following website: http://www.entrepreneurship.org/en/entrepreneurship-law/law-school-entrepreneurship-clinics.aspx.

FINANCIAL SUPPORT

In the starting phase of your organization, you may be able to provide services with little or no cost – primarily with board contributions and volunteers. However, as demand for your services increases, you will find that additional financial resources are needed to buy equipment, to hire professional help, to rent office space, and for other necessary expenses. At this point, a "resources development" plan is recommended to organize your fund raising efforts.

There are a number of issues to consider as you develop your plan, including:

- What type of funding do I need (e.g., capacity-building, programming, etc.)?

- Where can I find the type of funding I need (e.g., foundations, government, corporations, etc.)?

- How much money do I need (i.e., budgeting)?

- What expertise do I need to manage these resources?

We will discuss these and other issues surrounding the process of securing financial resources for your organization.

Fundraising – Embracing the Challenge

I haven't met too many people who LOVE fundraising. Just think about it...writing all those grants that don't get funded, smoozing the grant reps at all those fundraiser dinners and worrying whether you'll be able to pay your staff in the next three months can get OLD. You may ask "why can't I just DO the work instead of having to always FUNDRAISE?"

Well, it's one of the "hazards" of working for and leading a not-for-profit organization. There is a constant conflict between spending time providing services to your target market and spending time cultivating resources to provide those same services (and this doesn't include time for strategically planning for the future).

I found a quote from Winston Churchill that I think is appropriate – "Attitude is a little thing that makes a big difference." In other words, a positive attitude toward fundraising is an important step in accepting the fact that if you're going to do the work you've been called to do, you will have to plan and execute a fundraising strategy.

As the old saying goes, to the sailor without a plan, any wind is the right one. This is certainly true in fundraising. The first step in successful fundraising is developing a plan. This means designing action steps to diversify the funding of your organization.[x] In developing your fundraising plan, here are some suggested first steps:

1. Why are you raising money (e.g., salaries, programming, operations, etc.)?

2. How much money do you want to raise and over what period of time?

3. Do I have the capacity to manage these funds? For example, federal funds have much higher financial management requirements than individual contributors may.

4. Do I truly KNOW my programs are/can be successful? For example, have you done a needs assessment for your target market OR how will you assess whether your program is effective in addressing the needs.

5. Who do I approach to raise the necessary funds?

6. What other resources are out there that I can use other than money?

Answers to these and many other questions will help shape your fundraising plan and aid you in an even more important step – implementation!

How Much Money Do I Need?

We've all heard the expression "if you fail to plan, you plan to fail" …and this is certainly true when it comes to the operations of your non-profit organization. As in your personal life, planning for your organization's fiscal health is a vital element in making sure that, for example, your expected revenues exceed your expenses. In addition to determining how much money you REALLY need, a budget can help you in the execution of your organizational plan in general (e.g., how many employees do I need, should I buy or rent office space, etc.).

Before going further, it would be good to highlight some general terms that are often used[xi]:

- **Fund Accounting** – Non-profit organizations aren't in the business of making a profit (thus, its name), so they use an accounting system called *fund accounting*. Fund accounting groups financial data together into funds or accounts that share a similar purpose.

- **Revenue** – The amount of money that is brought into a company by its "business" activities (e.g., grants, income from programming, contributions, etc.).

- **Expense** – Any expenses incurred in the ordinary course of business (e.g., salaries, office space rental fees, taxes, etc).

- **Operating expenses** – A category of expenditure that a business incurs as a result of performing its normal business operations.

- **Non-operating expenses** – An expense incurred by activities not relating to the core operations of the business (e.g., interest charges or other costs of borrowing funds).

- **Cash-flow** – The cash generated from the operations of a company, generally defined as revenues less all operating expenses, but calculated through a series of adjustments to net income. NOTE: It is cash flow that pays the bills ("cash is king")!

The financial statements for non-profits relate to for-profit statements in the following way[xii]:

Business Financial Statement	Equivalent Non-profit Statement
Income Statement	Statement of Activities
Balance Sheet	Statement of Financial Position
Cash Flow	Statement of Cash Flows

Back to developing your budget... It is recommended that the following steps be taken to methodically develop your budget[xiii]:

1. List your monthly non-profit operational expenses.

2. List your monthly salaries and wages for each employee (if applicable).

3. Identify and list your monthly expenses for your specific programs.

4. Identify your monthly revenues.

5. Assess the difference between your monthly revenue and expenses.

Please make sure that you are *realistic* and *practical* in your planning so that expectations are not set too high. As with a for-profit business, sometimes an organization can get overwhelmed if it grows too fast too soon!

Different Types of Funding

After you've developed the budget for your organization, you will be in a better position to determine the type(s) of funding you will need. There is a tendency to only focus on the different SOURCES of funding that are available (which we'll cover in the near future) rather than recognizing and focusing on funding the different TYPES of needs you have.

In general, there are three primary expense types that require fundraising - operational, capital and programming. As mentioned previously, *operational expenses* are expenditures that a business incurs as a result of performing its normal business operations. Examples of operational expenses include salaries, office space, and supplies. *Capital expenses* are expenditures creating future benefits – for example, fixed assets such as a building, property or equipment.[xiv] One primary difference between operational and capital expenditures is how they are treated for tax purposes.

As you begin to research funding options, you'll discover that there are many more opportunities to secure funding for programs than there are for funding operations or capital purchases. This is because many funders are eager to support the functions that directly impact those whose needs are being met (i.e., programming) and place less of an emphasis on the "*in*direct" functions that support programming (e.g., salaries and buildings). However, as one who has been on both sides of the funding table, it is recognized that financial support for the people and assets that support programming is vital for long-term sustainability (there's only so much that volunteers can or would be willing to do!).

Important Tip:

Consider the funder's needs as you determine YOUR needs!

To address this need for financial support for operations, many funding sources allow for a percentage of the grant to be used for this purpose (typically, 10% of the grant amount). There are a few grantmakers that provide funding specifically for operational expenses (e.g., NC Community Development Initiative in North Carolina); however, most of them are housed within city and county governments where resources are scarce and needs are high. You may find that this amount is insufficient to cover all operational expenses, thus the need to identify additional funding sources.

Where Can I Find the Money?

When it comes to fundraising, knowing *where* to find the money is as important as *how* to get it. We've talked some about the "how" in the past, so now we'll provide a brief introduction to the "where."

There are five primary sources of funding for non-profits – individuals, foundations, federated funds, churches/organizations and government[xv].

- Individuals – Individual contributors make up the largest source of giving to non-profits and once they are contributors, they can become your most fervent advocates. However, one key disadvantage is the cost associated with developing and reaching these individuals, with a relatively small return per contributor.

- Foundations – According to the Foundation Center, there are more than 76,000 grantmaking foundations in the United States that give more than $40 billion in gifts annually. There are three types of foundations: community, corporate and independent.

- Federated Funds – A federated fund is a cooperative enterprise, owned and controlled by the non-profit members, whose purpose is raising program and operating capital for each member agency (e.g., United Way).

- Churches/Organizations - Depending on your organization's mission, churches and other organizations can become key partners in achieving your goals and objectives. These organizations are more likely to be a source for volunteers and other in-kind assistance.

- Government – While a great source for large sums of money, the application process and on-going compliance requirements can be time-consuming and arduous. To find out about federal government grants, go to www.grants.gov.

How Do I Get the Money?

We are all familiar with the famous quote from the movie *Jerry Maguire* – "Show me the money!" It means "put up or shut up"… do what you say you're going to do … walk the talk. When it pertains to raising funds for your organization, it is rare that someone will walk into your office and say "I have a million dollars to give to your organization" (it would be nice, but highly unlikely – unless you're close to Henry Ford or Bill Gates). Therefore, you have to SEEK out the funds and then do what it takes to SECURE those funds.

Whether it's a foundation or government grant, each has a process by which you communicate your funding needs as well as how your needs match the funder's priorities. There are a number of methods by which you can communicate your needs, including:

- Face-to-face – As you network in your community, you will meet different people who may have an interest in working with you to address your funding needs. Take the opportunity to tell them about your organization and, if appropriate, ask for a follow-up meeting to discuss your needs, including financial. The saying is true that people tend to help those whom they know. Also, you never know how a person may be able to help you – don't just focus on the money!

- Letter of introduction/interest – This is an effective way to introduce your organization to a potential funder without the pressure and time commitment associated with a formal application. In fact, many funders require this as a "pre-application" step to screen out ineligible requests before time and effort are spent by the applicant to complete a more detailed application.

- Formal application – Most funders use an application to obtain information about an applicant such as its organizational structure, its target audience, its programming, and its desired use of the funds being requested. More and more applications for funding are being completed and submitted on-line.

To talk a bit more about formal applications, there are some key pieces of information that are requested (many we've talked about before).

- Tax-exempt status – Many funders can only make contributions to organizations that have obtained tax-exempt status from the IRS. This means that contributions made to this type of organization are tax-deductible to the contributor and that many purchases made by the organization can be purchased tax-free. For more information on obtaining tax-exempt status for your organization, visit the IRS website.

- Evaluation – A funder wants to know that their contribution will have the desired impact that led them to make the contribution in the first place. To better ensure this, the application will request details up front on how the program will be evaluated to determine success. For example, if your goal is to reduce the number of students dropping out of school, how will you know you are successful (e.g., benchmarking, pre- and post-testing, etc.)? You may consider securing outside assistance from, say, a university to provide expertise and objectivity.

There are many other items included in formal applications for funding. However, if you are diligent in following the recommendations above as well as those giving previously, you will be better prepared to apply for and secure funding.

Who Can I Call For Help with My Finances?

By now you should have a general idea of how much money you need to operate and are aware of some funding sources that could contribute toward your efforts. However, there are still some key questions you should be able to answer, such as "who's going to actually write the grant applications?" or "what's the best way to account for these funds?" or "are there other requirements that come with this money and how do I handle them?"…among others.

A good start to answering these questions can be found in identifying some key persons and their associated tasks, including grant writers, grant managers, and bookkeepers/accountants.

Grant Writers - Just as the name implies, grant writers develop the grant package that is sent to potential funders and can assist in identifying other potential funders. In many organizations (especially start-ups), the organization's grant writer may also be the board chair or a congregant at the church or a student volunteer or… In any case, this person ensures that the organization and its programming are placed in the best light for the potential funder to see.

According to the American Association of Grant Professionals, freelance grant writers must guard against unethical behavior on the part of the organizations on behalf of which they write grants. Some organizations may try to pay a grant writer only after the grant has been awarded or pay the grant writer with a percentage of the grant money. According to the Association, both of these practices are ethics violations. Be mindful of this as you consider compensation for your grant writer.

Grant Managers - Consider this scenario: You got the grant! Everyone is thrilled…until reality hits. Someone has to be responsible for administering the project, complying with regulations, reporting to the funder…and that someone is (drumroll, please) the grant manager. Regardless of whether you are seasoned professional at a large institution or a volunteer for a grassroots organization, the job of a grant manager is a balancing act – making sure that program staff have the flexibility to accomplish something meaningful, while at the same time that every obligation to the funding source is met.[xvi]

Bookkeeper/Accountant - Starting out, you may be able to use Microsoft Excel or even a basic version of QuickBooks to account for revenues and expenses for your organization's administration and programming. However, as you secure greater amounts of funding from government and philanthropic sources, their compliance requirements may dictate that you seek out an experienced bookkeeper or accountant to report on the use of their funds. At a minimum, they may require an annual audit of your financing by an independent CPA which, depending on the size of your organization, can cost thousands of dollars.

In conclusion, make sure that your organization's financial plan includes not only raising funds, but properly managing and accounting for these funds as well.

Resources to Explore

Funding Sources/Information

- Community Foundations - (http://communityfoundations.net/)
- Chronicle of Philanthropy - (http://philanthropy.com/section/Home/172)
- Enterprise Community Partners - (http://www.enterprisecommunity.com/)
- Information of federal grants - (http://www.grants.gov)
- Local Initiatives Support Corporation (LISC) - (http://www.lisc.org/)
- Opportunity Finance Network - (http://www.opportunityfinance.net/)
- Urban Awareness USA - (http://www.urbanawarenessusa.org/)

THE IMPORTANCE OF LEADERSHIP

Before the first grant is ever written and the first staff person is hired, there is (or should be) a process that determines the organization's vision and mission as well as what the organization will do to fulfill its mission. Who drives this process? How are the vision, mission and goals/objectives determined? It takes dedicated and, yes, inspired people to come together and work toward addressing a community need, righting an institutional wrong, or giving a voice to the disenfranchised.

Leadership cannot be overstated as a vital element in the success of any effort, especially in community economic development (CED). Whether you're a visionary, an implementer, "out front" or "behind the scenes," leadership on all levels is needed for success. There are many definitions of leadership and quotes by famous people about leadership. However, I have found one leadership theory I like that suggests common traits and characteristics of leaders:

- **Honesty** – People want to follow an honest leader. Years ago, many employees started out by assuming that their leadership was honest simply because the authority of their position. This is no longer true. Leaders frequently miss the opportunity to display honesty when they mishandle addressing mistakes they have made.

- **Forward-Looking** – The whole point of leadership is figuring out where to go from where you are now. When people do not consider their leader forward-looking, that leader is usually suffering from one of two possible problems: (1) the leader doesn't have a forward-looking vision, or (2) the leader is unwilling or scared to share the vision with others. The leader may not trust their staff/people to "do it right," so nothing gets done.

- **Competence** – People want to follow someone competent. This doesn't mean a leader needs to be the foremost expert in every area, but they need to be able to demonstrate competency. Like the other traits, however, it isn't enough for a leader to be competent. They must demonstrate competency in a way that people notice. However, remember that a potential danger is that of minimizing others' contributions and appearing to take credit for the work others have done.

- **Inspiring** – People want to be inspired. In fact, there is a whole class of people who will follow an inspiring leader – even when the leader has no other qualities. Being inspiring means telling people how your organization is going to change the world (or, at least, your local community).

- **Intelligence** – Intelligence is something that can be difficult to develop. The road toward becoming more intelligent is difficult, long and can't be completed without investing considerable time. Developing intelligence is a lifestyle choice. To develop intelligence you need to dedicate yourself to continual learning – both formally and informally.

As you look to develop your own leadership style, always remember the ultimate goal for CED *(in my humble opinion)* – creating environments and situations where the community can best realize its own positive ends (socially, economically, politically, etc.).

Leadership Styles

When it comes to the topic of leadership, questions abound and opinions vary. What makes an effective leader? Are leaders "born" or "bred?" How can the same person be a "good" leader to one person and a "bad" leader to another? Throughout history, we find examples of how leadership can alter the course of the world – for good or bad (e.g., Moses, Jesus Christ, Adolph Hitler, Martin Luther King, Jr., etc.). However, these same leadership traits and styles can be found in our families, on our boards of directors, in our businesses, in governments…in all aspects of our life.

It is important to recognize (and appreciate) different styles of leadership that we use (and witness being used) to determine whether the style is the best choice to realize stated goals and objectives. In 1939, a psychological research study led by Kirt Lewin was conducted that identified three difference leadership styles – authoritarian, delegative, and participatory.[xvii]

Authoritarian - Authoritarian leaders provide clear expectations for what needs to be done, when it should be done, and how it should be done. There is also a clear division between the leader and the followers. Authoritarian leaders make decisions independently with little or no input from the rest of the group. Authoritarian leadership is best applied to situations where there is little time for group decision-making or where the leader is the most knowledgeable member of the group. However, it was found that decision-making was less creative under authoritarian leadership. In addition, it is more difficult to move from an authoritarian style to a democratic style than vice versa. Abuse of this style is usually viewed as controlling, bossy, and dictatorial. Conversely, authoritarian leadership comes when the leader doesn't really know what to do and is afraid to let people see it.

Delegative - Researchers found that the group that had delegative (laissez-fair) leadership was the least productive of all three groups. Group members made more demands on the leader, showed little cooperation and were unable to work independently. Delegative leaders offer little or no guidance to group members and leave decision-making up to group members. While this style can be effective in situations where group members are highly qualified in an area of expertise, it often leads to poorly defined roles and a lack of motivation.

Participatory - Participatory (or democratic) leaders offer guidance to group members, but they also participate in the group and allow input from other group members. Participative leaders encourage group members to participate, but retain the final say over the decision-making process. Group members feel engaged in the process and are more motivated and creative. It was found that groups led by these types of leaders were less productive than groups led by authoritarian leaders, but their contributions were of a much higher quality. Nevertheless, the study found that participatory leadership is generally the most effective leadership style.

Over time, other subcategories of leadership styles have been identified, including situational, emergent, transformational, strategic, and servant brands of leadership.

Even though leaders may emphasize (or feel comfortable with) one leadership style over another, it is important to recognize that, depending on the situation as well as to the people being led, leaders must be able to adjust their leadership style without compromising the five leadership traits given above.

What type of leadership style do you use? Which style do you think is the most effective? Who would you consider the best leader you know and why?

Leadership Structures

As you look to create or grow your organization, it is important to remember the vital role that leadership plays in the organization's success and that there are different leadership styles that can be used, depending on the situation at hand. Another important aspect of organizational development is the decision surrounding the organization's leadership structure. This decision of how the organization's leadership is structured goes a long way in determining whether goals and objectives can be realized effectively and efficiently.

__Important Tip:__

As you lead your organization, remember the Golden Rule (do unto others as you would have them do unto you)!

One definition of organizational leadership structure is "the intentional design of how the leadership communicates, enforces policy and provides feedback opportunities for its employees."[xviii] As with leadership styles, there are a number of leadership structures that can be considered. In fact, "style" and "structure" are closely aligned. In other words, the leadership structure that's used usually supports and enhances the leaders' style, whether it is authoritarian, participatory or delegative.

For most organizations focused on community economic development (CED), a board of directors is established to create structure, policies, and procedures that support good organizational governance. For start-ups, a "working" board also is charged with facilitating the day-to-day work needed to grow the organization. As monies are secured and programs begin to grow, the board typically hires an executive director to manage day-to-day operations who, in turn, hires additional staff as needed.

According to BoardSource, whose mission is to advance the public good by building exceptional non-profit boards and inspiring board service, these are the most frequent questions asked by board members regarding board organization::

- How can we contribute to effective board organization?

- How large should our board be?

- What should be the length of a board members' term?

- What committees should our board have?

The answers to these questions vary greatly and have direct (and possibly unintended) consequences. For example, if the number of board members is too small, the organization will not have the benefit of diverse skill sets to draw upon. However, if the number of board members is too large, decision-making could become cumbersome if not managed properly (e.g., establishment of committees). Many well-intentioned leaders/organizers overlook the likelihood that "tie" votes will occur if there is an even number of board members.

Equally important to the size of the board is that board members understand the roles of the board of directors and staff, particularly the executive director. As mentioned earlier, boards typically hire the executive director who, in turn, hires additional staff as needed. A thorough understanding and acceptance of the roles and responsibilities of the board and staff are needed to guard against "overlap." For example, a board member should not independently instruct a program director to perform a particular task. It is the executive director's responsibility to manage staff time and efforts in support of the organization's goals and objectives as directed by the board.

In conclusion, proper leadership structure can better support the effective work of the organization. Along with structure, it is important to understand and appreciate the different roles and responsibilities of each leadership level (i.e., board, executive director, and staff).

Do you serve on a board of directors or serve as a staff member? Is the organization as effective as it can be?

Resources to Explore

- BoardSource - (http://www.boardsource.org/)

The Personal Side of CED

We've discussed a number of topics pertaining to community economic development (CED) – from identifying key partners to embracing fundraising to recognizing the important role of the legal profession. However, we must not forget that at the end of the day, community economic development is a "people business." It takes <u>knowledgeable</u> people to create and implement policies and procedures that positively affect communities. It takes <u>observant</u> people to see how local decisions and regional trends will affect them and their communities. It takes a <u>giving</u> person to look beyond themselves and see how they can help improve their communities. In other words, the basic infrastructure for successful CED is made up of the development of the people who live in that community.

I will be the first one to admit that I am not a psychologist, sociologist or any other expert in the study of people. However, I believe there are a number of ways that individuals can prepare themselves physically, mentally and spiritually for the work of CED. A few are listed below:

- **<u>Gain knowledge</u>** – We've all heard that "knowledge is power," and this is especially true when it comes to CED. Individuals must become knowledgeable about issues such as available resources, trends in the economy, who to contact for assistance, and new laws that can affect your work. The more people who have relevant knowledge, the better.

- **<u>Get control of your personal finances</u>** - The issue of debt is something that people generally don't discuss because it's so personal and, sometimes, embarrassing. I've experienced personally how excessive debt can be an "albatross around your neck"! It can, for example, hinder your ability to support local businesses, one of the building blocks of CED. If you have better control of your personal finances, you will be in a better position to buy a home, expand your education or even start a business. For many years, Black Enterprise Magazine has led a campaign to encourage individuals and families to improve their financial status and has recently initiated a Financial Fitness Contest.

- **Give** - I believe that a person (and a community) that is focused on giving will generate not only goodwill, but increased resources as a result. The Bible speaks about giving numerous times throughout the text. Examples include the following:

    - "Give, and it will be given to you. A good measure, pressed down, shaken together and running over, will be poured into your lap. For with the measure you use, it will be measured to you" (Luke 6:38 NIV).

    - "'Bring all the tithes into the storehouse, That there may be food in My house, And try Me now in this,' Says the Lord of hosts, 'If I will not open for you the windows of heaven and pour out for you such blessing that there will not be room enough to receive it'" (Malachi 3:10 NKJV).

    - "But this I say: He who sows [plants, gives] sparingly will also reap [gather, gain] sparingly, and he who sows bountifully will also reap bountifully" (2 Corinthians 9:6 NKJV) [Comments added].

In short, a discussion of the "macro" issues of CED should begin with a discussion of what it takes to improve the health and wellbeing of those on the "micro" level – its people.

PUTTING IT ALL TOGETHER

We've discussed a number of topics related to developing your idea to address a need in your community and ways to organize your efforts to achieve your goals. It is my hope that these topics have been helpful to you as you begin and/or proceed on your journey. I may not have been as exhaustive in my information as you may need; however, these entries can be used as a launching pad to help guide you in your search for more information.

I readily admit that there are many professionals in this field that are more experienced that I am, but I have a passion for this work and this primer was one way to share my thoughts and more than 15 years of experience. I thank you for taking this journey with me and I pray that all of your efforts are successful.

And speaking of "your efforts"…are you ready to take the plunge? What's stopping you from moving forward? Nothing stops an idea better than inaction. **Just go for it!!**

BONUS ENTRIES

The following entries can be found on my blog - New South Blog (http://newsouthblog.wordpress.com).

A "Kingly" Service (posted on January 17, 2011)

Image of Selma to Montgomery march

One of the most interesting periods of history for me is the decade of the 1960s. It was a period of tremendous turmoil and growth in the country, both politically and culturally.

It was during this time that Dr. Martin Luther King, Jr. was a primary figure in shaping many of the decade's events. He showed that the collective faith and efforts of individuals, churches, and grassroots organizations can "move mountains" of racism, injustice and hopelessness.

One of the ways I plan to honor Dr. King's legacy is by continuously increasing my knowledge base to better assist communities to realize their full potential. *Question:* In what ways are you making your community better? In other words, what is your "kingly" service? Feel free to respond with your comments.

Autism and Economic Development (posted on April 2, 2011)

"What does autism have to do with economic development?" you might ask. Well, as it turns out, it does, and will continue to, have an effect. As with any trend, economic developers and other community leaders must be mindful of global, social, financial and even medical trends and how these trends affect their community's overall health and growth opportunities.

According to the Mayo Clinic, autism is one of a group of serious developmental problems called autism spectrum disorders (ASD) that appear in early childhood — usually before age 3. Though symptoms and severity vary, all autism disorders affect a child's ability to communicate and interact with others. Children with autism generally have problems in three crucial areas of development — social interaction, language and behavior.

Of course, for many of you, I'm "speaking to the choir." With 1 in nearly 100 children being diagnosed with autism, either your family or the family of someone you know has been affected (including my family).

So, back to the question at hand…how does autism and economic development relate? The children diagnosed with autism today will become, unless a cure is discovered, adults with autism tomorrow. As this occurs, communities that have the medical and (more importantly) social infrastructure to accommodate their needs will succeed in not only attracting them, but their families and other support networks.

In honor of Autism Awareness Month, take this opportunity to reflect on how your community recognizes, supports and assists in integrating those affected with autism and other developmental delays into the overall community. For more information on autism and other developmental delays, visit the websites of Autism Society, Autism Speaks and The Arc.

᳘

A "Tragedy" Brewing (posted on March 12, 2011)

Unless you've been "living under a rock" (a la GEICO), events in Libya, Egypt, and Japan as well as other areas in the Pacific are rocking the world in profound, historic ways. Each have at least one thing in common – there was very little warning to the average person of the events that occurred and the speed at which change happened. For example, it was reported that the waves from the tsunami resulting from the Japan earthquake traveled at more than **600 miles per hour** – faster than a commercial jet – and reached the west coast of the United States within a few short hours! I pray that democracy and peace prevail in the Middle East and that the rescue and recovery efforts go smoothly in Japan and elsewhere.

However, there is a "tragedy" that's brewing in the halls of Congress and other seats of power in the United States. The difference between this "tragedy" and the ones mentioned above is that we are being warned of what may occur. At this time, programs that assist those who are most vulnerable economically are being considered for massive budget cuts - programs such as the Community Development Block Grant (CDBG) program, Neighborhood Stabilization Program (NSP), and others. In North Carolina, funds that help support organizations that work within majority-minority communities are on the "chopping block" – not just for budget cuts, but are being "zeroed" out! This comes at a time when foreclosures continue to rise, unemployment rates are high and stagnant, and overall costs are rising (how much more are you spending to fill your car up?).

I recognize the need for all of us to "tighten our belts" during times of scarcity and that the burden and sacrifice should be borne equitably. However, it is a shame that programs such as the ones mentioned above and the communities they serve tend to bear the brunt of the burden during lean AND prosperous times (e.g., urban renewal in the '60s and '70s). I encourage you to learn about what's being considered and discussed at your local, state, and national government levels and get involved to make the change <u>you</u> want to see!

I hope that cooler heads prevail in that as budget talks proceed, that a disproportionate amount of sacrifice is not borne by those who can least afford it.

CED 101: A Primer

Tragedy Averted ... Maybe (posted on April 9, 2011)

Just before the federal government was scheduled to shut down, a deal was struck to keep the government "open for business," while implementing a spending package that has been described as "historic." I applaud the Herculean efforts of President Obama, House Speaker Boehner, Senate Majority Leader Reid and staff members in getting a deal done before the shutdown deadline.

I have to admit I have mixed emotions. On one hand, I'm happy for the hundreds of thousands of federal workers that would have been furloughed during a shutdown, including many of my colleagues. Talk that a prolonged government shutdown would have hindered the country's economic recovery has been put on the shelf. Services that many people rely on for everyday survival will continue (I hope!).

On the other hand, I'm cautious because as of the writing of this blog entry, few details of the spending plan have been made public. What programs are included in the $38 billion "cut" package? Who will bear the burden of these reductions? Will the economic recovery of those who are most in need be hindered? How will the faith-based and non-profit communities be affected?

As we've all heard before, the "devil's in the details." Oh, by the way, these discussions are only the beginning – negotiations on raising the debt ceiling and the 2012 federal budget loom just around the corner. It will continue to be interesting times – stay tuned!

What Do Elephants and Poverty Have in Common (posted on April 23, 2011)

The answer to the question posed in the title is not apparent…until I share with you a couple of books I read recently.

To Right These Wrongs by Robert Korstad & James Leloudis

I heard about this book on WUNC (our local NPR station) on a Saturday morning a number of months ago and was interested in buying it, but didn't at the time. I was re-introduced to the book at a recent meeting (thanks, Jeanne Tedrow!) and was encouraged to read it. To Right These Wrongs tells the story of the North Carolina Fund, described in the book's Introduction as "a pioneer effort to improve the lives of the 'neglected and forgotten' poor in a nation that celebrated itself as an affluent society," which was used as a "laboratory" in the mid-1960's for President Lyndon Johnson's Great Society and its war on poverty. This five-year effort brought together civic leaders – men and women, black and white – from across the state to work toward correcting the ills brought on by discrimination and poverty. Even though their efforts were groundbreaking and their lasting effects are still being felt today, they came to understand that it would take more than "charity and self-help" to alleviate poverty.

don't think of an elephant! by George Lakoff

If someone were to tell you "Now, don't think of an elephant. Whatever you do, DON'T THINK OF AN ELEPHANT!" What are you going to do...of course, think of an elephant! This book speaks to the importance of uniquely "framing" your message and that trying to use an opponent's message against them by using their "frames" only reinforces their message. An example of this is the use of the term "tax relief" for "tax cut." When you are "relieved" of something, this suggests that you were previously "burdened" and that, in this case, taxes are a burden to be relieved of. The question of what expenses get reduced (or how much debt to take on) to offset these tax reduction efforts (e.g., military vs. social programs) become the battleground issues. In fact, Democrats began using the term when trying to counteract the Republicans message, which only reinforced the need for "relief." Whether you are a Democrat or Republican, or consider yourself conservative, liberal or progressive, this book helps to show the importance of creating your own "frames of reference" in shaping your message.

Both these texts highlight the importance of creating effective policies for the "change you want to see," and developing effective communications and crafting a message that will accurately portray your mission, and contribute immensely to your level of success.

❧

Mother's Day Reflections (posted on May 7, 2011)

As I reflect on this Mother's Day, I want to celebrate my mother, Ruby Simmons Fuqua, and all of the mothers I had (and have) in my life (my grandmother, my aunt, my older (and younger) sister, the ladies at church and in the neighborhood, etc.). The "village" that raised me and supported me is extensive and diverse and I thank them ALL for the role they had in shaping my life.

Since 2004, I've had to reflect on my own mother without her being here on this side of life. This year, I think about the things that my mother taught me that led me to further develop an interest in and pursue a career in community economic development.

Entrepreneurship – When I started kindergarten, my mother "kept kids" for working families at our home. She not only wanted to earn extra income for our family, she wanted the flexibility to be available for my younger sister and me when we were in school. In fact, for some families, she provided babysitting services for more than one generation. My mother taught me to not be afraid of hard work and that owning your own business can provide freedom and flexibility.

Community Service – My exposure to community service began with seeing my mother and others support families in the neighborhood when important events happened (e.g., marriages, deaths, graduations, etc.). That support helped to strengthen, unify and stabilize the neighborhood. In today's time, with the increased mobility of families, neighborhood support and community service has become more and more "corporate" in nature (e.g., neighborhood associations). However, no matter the structure (home-grown vs. corporate), the same results are desired – strong, unified and stable communities. My desire for community service is a direct result of my early observations of the work of my mother and others.

Education – Even though my mother did not finish high school, she was a strong supporter of my educational pursuits. In fact, to this day I remember that it was my mother that taught me how to multiply 100 and 100 (multiply the numbers in front of the zeros (1 x 1) and then add the number of zeros (4) to the end of the multiplied number to get the answer – 10,000) and how to spell "comfortable" (Com – For – Table). She taught me that difficult challenges can be addressed by looking at the problem in smaller components and addressing them one by one.

Take this time to reflect on the positive lessons your mother (and those that represented motherhood) taught you and use them in your service for the betterment of your community.

Labor Day Reflections (posted on September 3, 2011)

According to the U.S. Department of Labor, Labor Day is a creation of the labor movement and is dedicated to the social and economic achievements of American workers. It constitutes a yearly national tribute to the contributions workers have made to the strength, prosperity, and well-being of our country.[xix]

As we approach the Labor Day holiday, I can't help but to think about how blessed I am to be employed. I would consider myself a "modern-day employee" in that for much of my career history, I sought out opportunities to expand my skill set either through a new position with my present employer, with a new employer or through entrepreneurship. With this strategy, I have been blessed to have gained a wide variety of experiences, with a primary focus on community and economic development. Nevertheless, there have been times when, unfortunately, I did not receive a steady paycheck or the entrepreneurial pursuit did not turn out as I expected. Through it all, God provided for me and my family and I thank Him for that!

I, also, can't help but to reflect on those who are unemployed or underemployed. As of this writing, the unemployment rate in the U.S. stands at 9.1% (August 2011). There are more than 13 million people who are seeking full-time employment, but have been unsuccessful for a number of reasons (e.g., jobs moving to lower cost locations, skills mismatch, etc.). This has implications for all areas of the economy, including homeownership, meeting basic needs, obtaining the training needed for today's jobs, and others. With the current direction of federal and state governments to reduce spending at all costs, the work and mission of non-profits become even more important. Non-profits have to become even more efficient in their operations and programming to address the ever-increasing needs of its target population, constituency and community.

Do not become discouraged in the present state of affairs, but rather use this time to be more creative in meeting the need and more emboldened in requesting and securing assistance for your efforts.

Please pray with me that the unemployed, employers, government leaders, non-profits and other willing participants will work together to improve our economy and increase meaningful opportunities!

Proud Dad (posted on October 8, 2011)

As I write this entry, our family is preparing to witness our son participate in a horse-riding competition. For most parents, attending competitions is an honored ritual – supporting our children as they prepare to succeed, compete with honor, and grow to become the productive citizens we pray they will be. But this is not just an ordinary contest – the contestants have overcome not just learning how to ride, but how to perform many everyday tasks we take for granted.

Now I can't speak for every competitor because I don't know them personally, but because this competition is geared toward those with special needs, I can only imagine what they may have had to overcome. As for our son, he continues to recover from autism slowly but surely. We thank God for the resources and people He has brought into our life to assist him (and his proud mom and dad!).

I wanted to take this opportunity to "swell my chest" for my son AND daughter as they continue to mature in this thing called LIFE. For those with children (biological, step, grand and otherwise), in the midst of serving your communities, congregants and constituents, show love to your children in any way you can (especially pray for them) – we don't have them for long!

[i] Marcia L. Colish, *Medieval Foundations of the Western Intellectual Tradition, 400-1400,* (New Haven: Yale Univ. Pr., 1997), p. 267.

[ii] Excerpts from article entitled *Marquette Joins in Creating Future of Milwaukee's Near West Side;* Association of Jesuit Colleges and Universities; Steve Schultz, Assistant Director of University Communication, Marquette University; May 2005 (Source: http://office.ajcunet.edu/connections/display.asp?issue=29&article=9&backissue=open)

[iii] Source: http://www.coas.howard.edu/hucup/about_commdevprojects.htm

[iv] Source: Community Wealth.org

[v] Source: Wikipedia.org

[vi] Author unknown (Source: http://www.quotegarden.com/names.html)

[vii] Source: Wikipedia (http://en.wikipedia.org/wiki/Needs_assessment)

[viii] Quote by Cullin Hightower

[ix] Gajda, Rebecca & Jennifer Jewiss (2004). Thinking about how to evaluate your program? these strategies will get you started. Practical Assessment, Research & Evaluation, 9(8). Source: http://pareonline.net/getvn.asp?v=9&n=8

[x] Source: Compassion Capital Fund (http://www.ccfbest.org/fundraising/)

[xi] Source: Investopedia.com

[xii] Source: http://tinyurl.com/3vyre8h

[xiii] Source: eHow.com

[xiv] Source: Wikipedia.com

[xv] Source: managementhelp.org

[xvi] Source: Essentials of Grant Management: A Guide to the Perplexed by Henry Flood (2001). Article can be found at http://www.tgci.com.

[xvii] Source: About.com (http://psychology.about.com/od/leadership/a/leadstyles.htm)

[xviii] Source: eHow.com

[xix] U.S. Department of Labor
(http://www.dol.gov/opa/aboutdol/laborday.htm)